Macmillan Bible Stories

LEVEL 2

Jesus Begins God's Work

retold by
CAROL CHRISTIAN

MACMILLAN

© Copyright text Carol Christian 1996
© Copyright illustrations Macmillan Education Ltd 1996

All rights reserved. No reproduction, copy or transmission of this publication may be made without written permission.

No paragraph of this publication may be reproduced, copied or transmitted save with written permission or in accordance with the provisions of the Copyright, Designs and Patents Act 1988, or under the terms of any licence permitting limited copying issued by the Copyright Licensing Agency, 90 Tottenham Court Road, London W1P 9HE.

Any person who does any unauthorised act in relation to this publication may be liable to criminal prosecution and civil claims for damages.

First published 1996 by
MACMILLAN EDUCATION LTD
London and Basingstoke
Associated companies and representatives in Accra, Banjul, Cairo, Dar es Salaam, Delhi, Freetown, Gaborone, Harare, Hong Kong, Johannesburg, Kampala, Lagos, Lahore, Lusaka, Mexico City, Nairobi, São Paulo, Tokyo

ISBN 0–333–63934–0

10   9   8   7   6   5   4   3   2
05   04   03   02   01   00   99   98   97   96

Printed in Hong Kong

A catalogue record for this book is available from the British Library.

Illustrations by Francis Phillips/Linden Artists Ltd

The Bible tells us that Jesus of Nazareth began his work about two thousand years ago.

He travelled from town to town, in the region of Lake Galilee, preaching to crowds of people, teaching the Word of God, and healing those who were sick. Many people believed that he was sent by God to save them from sin and death.

But first Jesus got ready to do God's work. He received a clear message from God when he was baptised and he stood firm against the temptation to serve the devil.

Jesus goes to John to be baptised

Jesus grew up in the town of Nazareth with his mother Mary and her husband Joseph, a carpenter. Jesus probably worked as a carpenter, too, when he was a young man.

However, Jesus was different from the people around him. He had special gifts. He studied the Jewish holy books, the Scriptures, and learned much of them by heart. He was strong, gentle and kind. He became a *rabbi*, or teacher. People came to him for help and felt better after talking with him.

When he was about thirty, there were reports of a new prophet in Judea. Everyone was talking about him. His name was John and he was preaching to great crowds of people, who followed him wherever he went.

Mary said, 'That's my cousin Elizabeth's son! His father was Zechariah, the priest. Even before he was born, we knew he was going to be a man of God.'

'He's a very holy man,' said a neighbour. 'He tells his followers to change their ways. He tells them to give away their food and clothes to people who don't have any. Every day he baptises lots of people in the River Jordan, to wash away their sins.'

Everyone passing the carpenter's shop stopped to talk about John. They called him 'John the Baptist'. Jesus listened eagerly.

'John's a strange man,' they told him. 'He's not like us. He dresses in camel skins and lives on honey and locusts. He doesn't eat and drink with his friends as other people do. Yet people say he is the Christ.'

All Jewish people were waiting for the Christ to come and save the world. The Scriptures promised he would come one day.

'He has plenty of courage. He tells the Roman soldiers and the tax collectors to treat people justly,' said one man. Everyone hated the Roman soldiers and the tax collectors. They robbed the people of the little money they had.

'Then the tax collectors ask him to baptise them!' exclaimed another, laughing. 'When they hear John preach, they really want to become better people.'

Jesus's heart beat faster when he heard what John was doing. The time had come for him to go out into the world to do God's work.

His family were not surprised when Jesus left home. They knew that God was calling him. He had to obey that call.

Jesus travelled down through the hills of Galilee and the valley of the River Jordan towards Jericho. Many of the people he met on the road were talking about John the Baptist.

'He's a great prophet,' they said. 'He walks with God. He doesn't want anything for himself. But he says he's not the Christ. He's preparing us to meet the Christ when he comes. He baptises us with water, but someone is coming who will baptise us with the Holy Spirit. That's what he says.'

'He's as brave as a lion,' one man said. 'He treats kings and beggars the same. "You're a sinner," he told King Herod. Perhaps we are all sinners.'

'That's true. We do bad things,' said another, 'but with God's help we can change.'

Some of the travellers said, 'John has washed away our sins. He's a truly holy man. He'll make the people of Israel into a better nation.'

Jesus came to the place on the River Jordan where John was baptising the people. He joined the crowd on the banks of the river.

Over the heads of the crowd he could see the thin figure of John in his rough, camel's hair tunic. He was lowering people into the river and asking God to bless them before raising them up again out of the water. Jesus joined those who were moving forward to be baptised.

John lifted the man ahead of him out of the water. Then he saw Jesus coming towards him. His heart gave a jump. A shock ran through him. 'That's him!' he said to himself. 'That's the one we have been waiting for!'

He called out to Jesus, 'Have you come to me? It is you who should baptise me!' He turned to the people around them and said, 'This is the man I told you about, who will baptise you with the Holy Spirit.'

John lowered Jesus into the River Jordan. As he came up, the sky above him opened and he saw the Holy Spirit flying down in the shape of a dove.
A voice from Heaven said, 'You are my dear son, and I am very pleased with you.'

Jesus heard God's call very clearly. He decided to go into the desert to be alone with God. He needed to think about what kind of work God wanted him to do, and to prepare himself to serve him.

Jesus is tempted by the devil

The River Jordan runs straight from the north to the south of Israel. It passes down through Lake Galilee. Then it flows on until, at last, it empties itself into the Dead Sea. The Dead Sea is so salty nothing can live in it.

In this region there is a dry, rocky desert. Nothing lives there but a few wild animals and birds.

After he was baptised, Jesus, full of the Holy Spirit, went into the desert and stayed there for forty days. He was waiting for another message from God, his father. He had nothing to eat and grew very hungry.

Then he heard a voice. It said to him, 'If you're the Son of God, you can do anything. Look at those stones at your feet. You're hungry. Why don't you turn them into bread? Then you can eat.'

Jesus felt the power of God inside him. He could do what the voice said. Yet he knew it wasn't God's voice that was speaking to him. It was the voice of God's enemy, the devil. Jesus wanted God to speak to him.

Then he remembered what he had learned from the holy books. He answered, 'The Scriptures tell us that we need more than bread when we are hungry. We need God's word.'

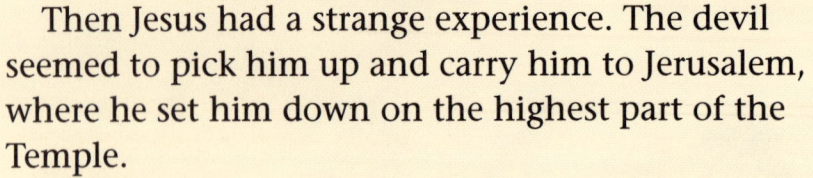

Then Jesus had a strange experience. The devil seemed to pick him up and carry him to Jerusalem, where he set him down on the highest part of the Temple.

He said to him, 'If you're the Son of God, prove it to me. Throw yourself down from here. You won't hurt yourself. You know what the Scriptures say. God will send his angels to catch you and keep you safe from harm. They won't let you fall. You won't even strike your foot against a stone.'

Jesus thought to himself, 'That's true. The Scriptures do say that.'

He was standing high above Jerusalem and there were crowds of people down below.

He thought to himself, 'If I throw myself down and the angels catch me, everyone will know that I am the son of God. They will worship me and listen to every word I say.'

However, he said to the devil, 'The Scriptures also tell us not to test the Lord our God.'

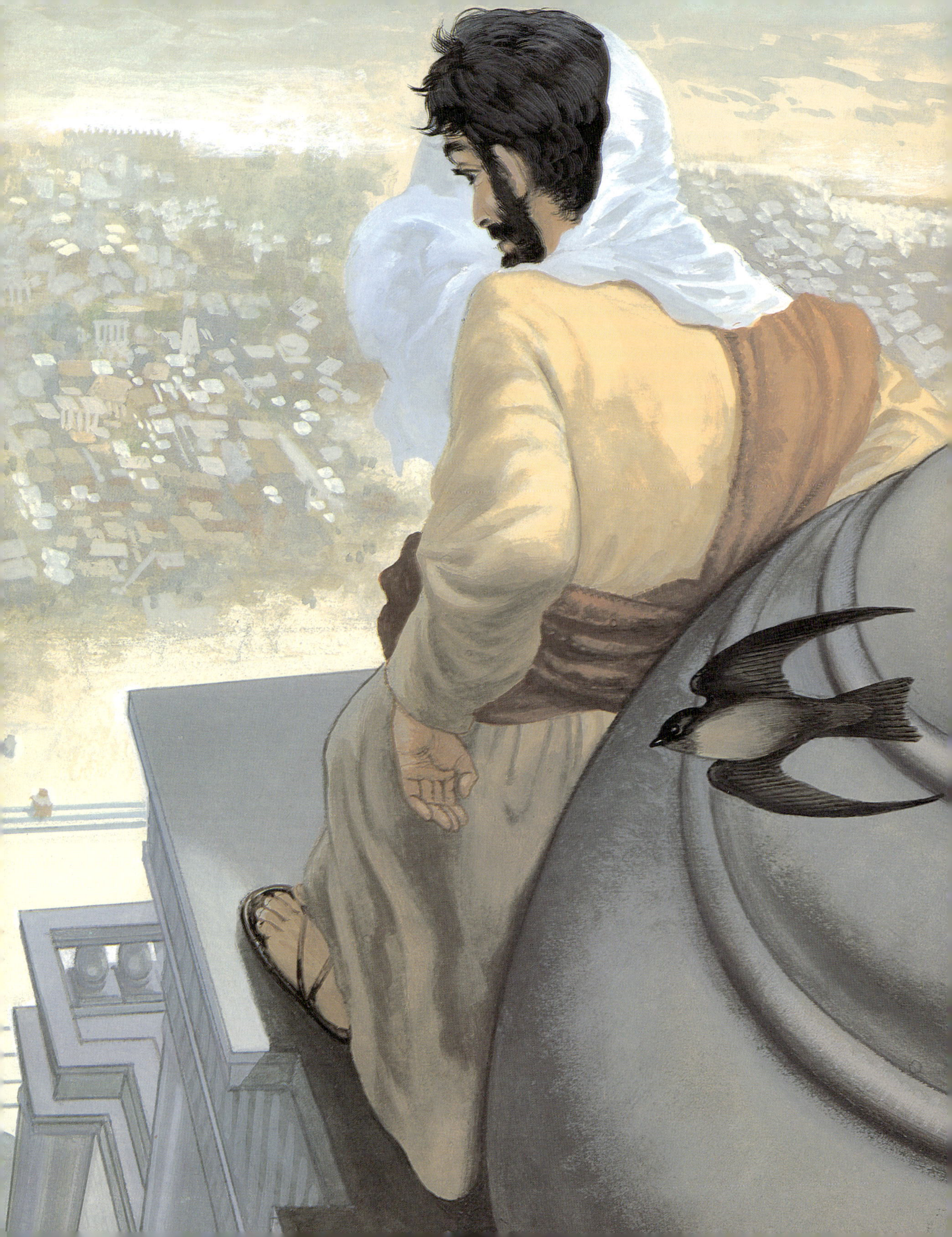

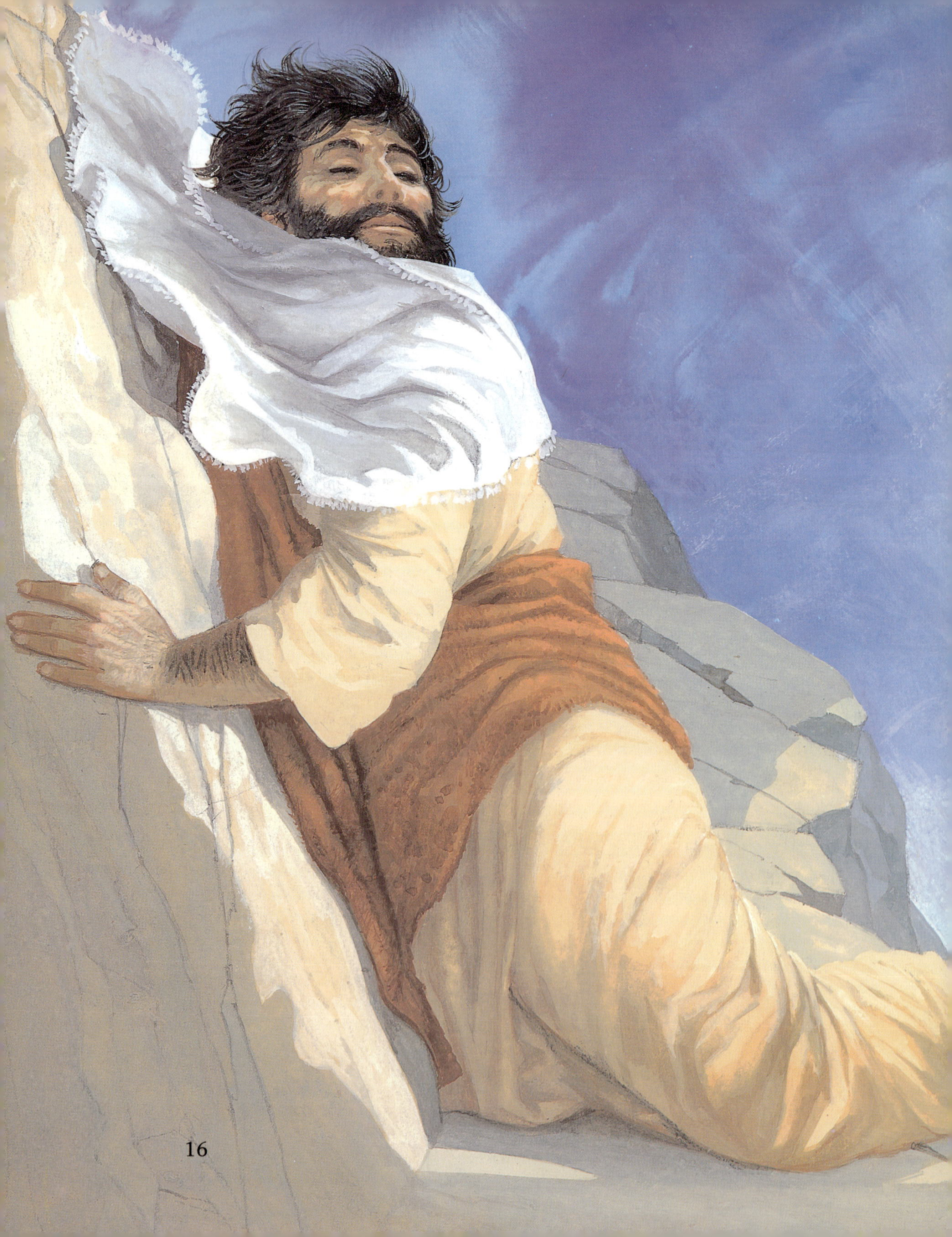

So the devil tried again. He took Jesus to the top of a very high mountain. From there, Jesus could see the whole earth. All the nations of the world were spread out before him.

The devil said to him, 'Look at the nations. Shall I give them to you? You can rule over them all, if you will fall down on your knees and worship me.'

Jesus looked down on the nations of the world. If he became the ruler of all the nations, he could bring them peace. There would be no more wars.

But Jesus knew very well that it was just another trick. 'Go away from me!' he said. 'The Scriptures tell us to worship God and no one else. We must never serve anyone but him.'

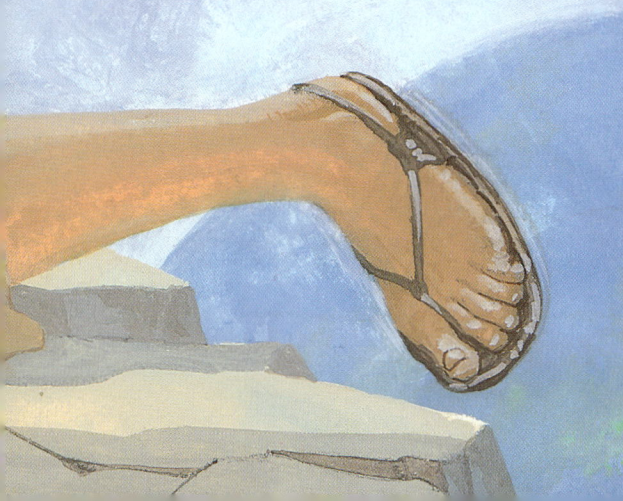

At last, Jesus found himself alone in the desert. The devil was gone. He was still hungry. He wasn't famous. He wasn't the ruler of even one nation. But he felt strong. He had fought with the devil and won. He loved God more than he loved food, or fame, or power. He would serve God.

Jesus chooses his first disciples

When Jesus returned from the desert, people told him, 'King Herod got angry with John the Baptist and has thrown him into prison. It isn't safe to speak the truth any more.'

He returned to the town of Capernaum, in Galilee, and began preaching to the people there. He told them, 'Change your hearts and lives. Be ready, because the Kingdom of Heaven is coming soon.'

One day, he was standing on the shore of Lake Galilee, teaching the people. There were so many people wanting to hear him that they were pushing him to the very edge of the water.

Jesus spoke to some fishermen, who were cleaning their nets nearby. Two of their boats were pulled up on the shore. One of the owners was a big, friendly man.

'May I climb onto your boat, Simon?' he asked.

'Yes, Master,' the man answered. 'I'll push it out into the water a little way.'

Jesus climbed onto it and sat down in the prow. Now everyone could see and hear him. The boat made a fine pulpit.

21

When he had finished teaching the people, he was tired. He said to Simon, 'Let's go out on the lake and catch some fish.'

Simon answered, 'We went fishing last night, Master, and didn't catch anything. But I suppose, if you want us to, we can try again.'

Simon's brother Andrew joined them. They rowed out into deep water and let down their nets. They didn't expect to catch anything but, when they pulled on their nets, they couldn't lift them into the boat. The nets were so full of fish they were beginning to tear.

They called to their friends, James and John, who were in the other boat with their father, Zebedee.

'Come and help us pull in the fish,' they called.

Their friends came at once and helped them pull in the nets. When they got them on board, both boats nearly sank from the weight of the fish.

Simon was amazed, but he was also afraid. 'Jesus isn't a fisherman,' he thought. 'How did he know where the fish were? Only God knew that.'

He looked at Jesus more closely. 'Can this man be God?' he wondered. Then he fell on his knees and cried, 'Leave me, Lord, for I am a sinner!'

Jesus smiled at him and said, 'Don't be afraid, Simon. From now on you will come fishing with me for the hearts of men.'

They returned to the shore and unloaded the fish. When their boats were safely tied up, Simon and his brother Andrew, and James and John, the sons of Zebedee, left their work and went to follow Jesus.

These men were his first followers, or 'disciples'. Simon was big and strong and very loyal to his friends. Jesus gave him the name 'Peter', which means 'rock'.

Jesus changes water into wine

Jesus soon had many disciples, both men and women. Twelve of them went everywhere with him. Simon Peter, Andrew, James and John were among them. They were eager to learn more about God, and Jesus taught them whenever he could.

One day Jesus and his disciples went to a wedding in the village of Cana. Cana wasn't far from his home in Nazareth and his mother Mary was also one of the guests.

Jesus enjoyed parties. He saw plenty of sickness and sadness in the crowds who followed him everywhere he went. At the wedding, he could join his family and friends for one of those happy occasions when people eat and drink and laugh together, and forget their troubles.

The bridegroom, who was their host, was generous to the people who came to his wedding. They drank so much wine that soon there was none left. He and his servants were ashamed when they saw that they had no more wine to offer to the wedding guests.

Mary was sorry for them. 'They have no more wine,' she said to her son. Her eyes were full of hope. She wanted Jesus to do something.

Jesus had refused to turn the stones at his feet into bread when he was hungry. He was reluctant to use God's power in this way.

He said, 'Don't tell me about it, Mother. My time hasn't come yet.'

But Mary felt sure he would do something. She said to the servants, 'Do whatever he tells you to do.'

Six large stone jars stood nearby. They held the water Jews used for washing before taking part in their religious ceremonies. Jesus said to the servants, 'Fill those jars right up with water.'

So the servants filled the jars with water. Then Jesus said, 'Pour some out and take it to the master of the feast.'

The master of the feast didn't know where the wine had come from, but the servants knew. When he had tasted it, he called to the bridegroom and said, 'People usually serve the best wine to their guests at the beginning of the feast. Then, when the guests have had a lot to drink, they serve the cheaper wine. But you have saved the best wine until now.'

The servants poured out wine for everyone. The bridegroom was glad, which made Mary glad, too. The wedding feast was a happy occasion right to the end.

Jesus heals a man who could not walk

The news about Jesus spread to all the towns and villages of Galilee. 'John the Baptist is in prison, but there is a new prophet, Jesus of Nazareth,' people said. 'He's not just a preacher. He's healing people, and driving evil spirits out of them.'

One day he was in a house in Capernaum. So many people gathered around him that no one could get in through the door. There were crowds outside the windows.

Four men came to the house, bringing a friend. They were carrying him on a mat because he couldn't walk. They wanted Jesus to heal him.

When they reached the house, they couldn't get in. They knew Jesus was there, but there was such a crowd, they couldn't see him or get near him. They had come a long way and felt very disappointed.

However, like many houses in Galilee, the house had a flat roof. It was made of mud, mixed with sticks and dry grass. The family sat out there on hot nights. Sometimes they slept there.

So the men climbed the steps that led up onto the roof. They cut out pieces of the roof to make a hole. Then they made the hole bigger. Soon the hole was as big as the man on the mat. They were able to lower their friend down through the hole into the space by Jesus's feet.

It was a surprise for the people down below! Bits of the roof fell on their heads, and faces looked down through the hole.

Jesus stopped speaking and looked up at the men on the roof. Their eyes were full of hope and trust. They were sure he was going to heal their friend. They trusted him completely.

Jesus looked down at the man on the mat. 'Young man,' he said to him, 'your sins are forgiven.'

Some teachers of the law were sitting there. They thought, 'How can he say that? Only God can forgive sins.'

Jesus knew what they were thinking. He asked them, 'What's wrong? Is it easier to say "Your sins are forgiven"? Or to say "Stand up, pick up your mat, and go home"?'

He was telling them something that they probably knew already. Sometimes people cannot walk because they have done something wrong and need God's forgiveness.

When the teachers of the law did not answer, Jesus added, 'But perhaps you do not believe that God has given me the power to forgive sins.'

Then he said to the man lying at his feet, 'I tell you, stand up, pick up your mat, and go home.'

At once, the man rose to his feet. Everyone watched as he bent down, picked up his mat, and walked out of the house, praising God.

The people were all amazed. They praised God, too, and said, 'We've seen some strange things here today!'

Jesus blesses the children

Jesus's disciples tried to protect him from the crowds. They saw how tired he became, and they knew he couldn't deal with everyone. They tried to bring him the people who needed his help most, or were most important.

One day some parents brought their children to Jesus. They didn't need help. Their parents just wanted Jesus to lay his hands on them and give them his blessing.

Jesus loved children but the disciples barred their way. The children were making a lot of noise and people couldn't hear what Jesus was saying.

'Go away! Don't waste the master's time,' they scolded. 'Can't you see how busy he is?'

Jesus was preaching to the people about the love of God. When he saw what his disciples were doing, he grew angry. He called out to them, 'Let the children come to me. Don't stop them. Children show us what God's kingdom is like.'

And he said to the people, 'We must trust in the Kingdom of God as children do, if we want to be his people. It's a terrible sin to harm one of these little ones.'

The children were listening now. They felt important. The disciples made a path through the crowd for them, and their parents brought them to Jesus, who took them in his arms and blessed them.

Jesus feeds the five thousand

One morning, when Jesus was teaching the people, his disciples came to him and said, 'John the Baptist is dead, killed by Herod's men. His disciples are here and would like to speak with you.'

Jesus was very sad, for John was a good and holy man. He went to speak with John's disciples. They told him, 'King Herod was afraid of John because the people listened to him. Now he is afraid of you, too, because you are calling the people to God. He believes that John is not dead but is alive in you. We've come to warn you. Be careful! He wants to destroy you.'

After they had gone, Jesus said to his disciples, 'Get a boat ready. We'll cross the lake to a quiet place where we can be alone for a while.'

Because so many people came to see Jesus, he spent very little time alone with his disciples. Sometimes they hardly had time enough to eat their meals.

They sailed across the lake to an empty hillside far from any town, where they could share a meal together and rest. However, when the people saw them go, they ran after them along the shore, reaching the place ahead of them.

When Jesus stepped ashore, he found a crowd waiting for him. His disciples wanted to send them away. 'We'll tell them you're tired. You've received bad news and are feeling sad. We'll say that you need rest. The people will understand,' they said.

But Jesus felt sorry for the people. They needed him so badly! 'They're like sheep without a shepherd,' he said. 'They don't know what to do or where to go.'

He stayed with them and taught them. He healed those who were sick. Late in the afternoon, his disciples went to him and said, 'It's getting late and this is a lonely place. Send the people away so they can go to the villages and farms and buy something to eat before it gets dark.'

Jesus answered, 'They don't need to do that. Give them something to eat here.'

His disciples didn't understand. They asked, 'Shall we go and buy bread for all these people? It will cost a great deal of money.'

'How many loaves have we got?' Jesus asked them.

They answered, 'We have five loaves of bread and two fish, but there are thousands of hungry people here.'

Jesus said, 'Give me what you have.'

He invited the crowd to sit down on the grass in groups of fifty and a hundred people. Then he blessed the bread and fish and broke them into pieces. He gave the pieces to his disciples to share out among the people.

Even his disciples couldn't understand what happened next. They took the pieces of bread and fish which Jesus gave them – there weren't very many – and when they offered them to the groups of people who were seated on the hillside, there was enough food for them all. Everyone took some and everyone got enough to eat.

When the disciples told the story later, not many people believed them. They themselves were still very puzzled. For, they said, 'When everyone finished eating, there were enough pieces left to fill twelve baskets! Yet more than five thousand people were on the hillside that day.'

Jesus walks on the water

Jesus said to his disciples, 'Get in the boat and go across the lake to Bethsaida, while I send the people home. I'd like to be alone for a little while.'

When everyone had gone, he went up into the hills to pray. Later, when it was dark, he came down and stood on the shore alone. The boat was a long way out and he could see that his disciples were in trouble. A strong wind was blowing and they were rowing against the wind.

Jesus went quickly towards them across the water. He was about to pass them and go on to the other side when they saw him and cried out, terrified. They thought he was a ghost.

He called out to them, 'Don't be afraid. It's me. I'm here.'

They felt much safer when they heard his voice. Peter answered, 'Lord, if it's really you, tell me to come to you across the water, and I'll come.'

So Jesus said, 'Come.'

Peter climbed over the side of the boat and started across the water towards Jesus. He started out bravely but, when he saw the power of the wind and the height of the waves, he got frightened and began to sink.

Thinking he was going to drown, he cried out, 'Lord, save me!'

Jesus reached out his hand and caught him. 'Oh, Peter,' he said, 'don't you trust me? Have you no faith in me?'

Suddenly the wind stopped blowing and the water of the lake grew calm. The moon shone through the clouds.

Their friends held out their hands to help them climb into the boat. When they were safe on board, the disciples fell at Jesus's feet, saying, 'Master! You really are the Son of God!'

Macmillan Bible Stories

Level 1

Adam and Eve

Noah

Jonah

Moses in Egypt

Jesus is Born

The Good Samaritan and
The Wise and the Foolish Bridesmaids

Level 2

Joseph

Ruth

When Jesus was a Boy

Jesus Begins God's Work
> *This story tells of the baptism and temptation of Jesus, the draught of fishes, the wedding feast at Cana, the healing of the lame man, the blessing of little children and the feeding of the five thousand.*

Lost but Found
> The Lost Sheep
> The Lost Coin
> The Prodigal Son

Jesus Dies and Lives Again